Raw Soups Salads and Smoothies

Simple Recipes for Everyday Health

by Frédéric Patenaude

> NOTE: This was first published in 2003. Because the author's research has evolved over the years, some of the nutritional concepts in this book may be in slight conflict with some of his newer research. However, these are for details and the basic philosophy stays the same. We hope that the reader will get great value from the content of this book, and will understand that the author's thoughts have been further defined in his next books.

Cover art: Martin Mailloux
www.mayoodesign.com

Copyright © 2003-2012 by Frédéric Patenaude
All rights reserved
No part of this publication may be reproduced, in any form or by any means, electronic, mechanical, photocopying, or otherwise, without prior written permission from the publisher.

First Edition, May, 2003
Printed in Canada
Second edition, January, 2012
Printed in the United States of America by CreateSpace

Published by:

Raw Vegan
358-1917 W 4th Ave
Vancouver, BC V6J1M7
Canada
For Support: www.replytofred.com

Acknowledgments: The author would like to thank his friends and family for testing his recipes and giving him their honest, sometimes brutal feedback. Without them, that mango-tomato smoothie would have made it into the book (Hey, I thought it was good!). Special thanks to Martin Mailloux, my favorite graphic designer, who comes up with exactly what I want every time. (Chapeau, mon cher Martin). Special thanks also to Surya for her patience and her spirulina smoothie that, unfortunately, I had to improve to include in the book
(la mangue change vraiment tout!).

This book is dedicated to all the people who grow the food that we eat.

Contents

Simple recipes? Why?	5
Description of Some of the Ingredients Used in This Book	5
What Seasonings to Use? What Seasonings to Avoid?	9
Raw Soups	11
How to Make Raw Soups	12
What Blender to Use	15
How Does it Work?	15
Raw Soup Recipes	17
How to Make a Great Salad	26
Salad Recipes	29
Smoothies	37
What Goes into a Smoothie?	38
Smoothies Recipes	39
Extra Section: Raw Dips	46
About the Author	50

Simple Recipes? Why?

Eating raw and living foods is a healthy, simple lifestyle choice. We eat raw fruits and vegetables because we want more energy, because we want to enjoy better health, because we want to have more concentration — in other words, because we want our lives to be less complicated. On a mostly or completely raw diet, we don't have to spend hours in front of the stove every day, preparing complex, unhealthy food. Instead, we can make a meal in less than ten minutes out of a few ingredients.

The question I am ofetn asked is: "Do you have a simple, raw food recipe book? I don't have much time to prepare anything complicated. I just want some simple recipes that taste good." This booklet is my answer to that question. *Raw soups, salads and smoothies* are the three main types of raw meals, when we are not just eating fresh, whole fruits and vegetables, nuts and seeds.

So, I offer herein this little book recipes for raw soups, salads and smoothies. They are healthy, easy to digest, and indeed simple. They can serve as examples for your own recipes — the ones that you'll be inventing on the spot with local, organic, seasonal ingredients.

Description of Some of the Ingredients Used in This Book

- **Black Olives, Sundried** — I use sundried, black olives that I buy at health food stores, through mail-order companies, or at Italian and Middle-Eastern markets. They have a strong and slightly bitter taste. I use them only occasionally because they contain a lot of salt. They are used in some recipes of this book as a seasoning.

- **Dulse** — Dulse is a sea vegetable. It can be bought whole (in leaves), in flakes, or powdered. I use dulse to give a salty flavor to soups and salads. This ends up being a better choice than using sea salt. Dulse flakes, for example, are slightly salty and the salt they contain naturally comes from the ocean. While it is not the best thing to add too much salt to food, the amount of salt contained in the recipes of this book (through the use of dulse or otherwise) is small.

- **Durian** — Durian is a spiky, stinky, delicious tropical fruit. It is bigger than a football. Durian is available at Asian markets, fresh or frozen. Fresh, it is quite expensive. You can buy it frozen and let it thaw overnight. Eating a durian for the first time is an experience — sort of comparable in intensity to a first kiss! To avoid disappointments, make sure you get a good one. Ask the experts at the Asian market to pick a ripe one for you.

- **Kalamatha Olives** — This is a variety of reddish olives available in many markets and health food stores.

- **Olive Oil** — It is preferable to limit the quantities of fat in the diet. So when using oil such as olive oil, only use a little bit to add flavor, but don't drown the vegetables in it. Good quality olive oil has a nice flavor, but you can also use other types of cold-pressed oil. Be also aware that you won't find good quality olive oil in your supermarket or even in many health food stores. The labels "extra-virgin" or "cold-pressed" don't mean a lot these days. So what are the options? Buy olive oil from mail-order companies or specialty shops such as Italian markets or good health food stores. Paying less than $8 for one liter of good quality olive oil is suspicious. Stone-pressed olive oil is probably the best.

- **Mature Coconut** — Mature coconuts are the brown coconuts we see at supermarkets. They have been picked ripe. The meat they contain is hard and oily. It is best to buy them at Asian or Hispanic markets. Those found in most supermarkets are too old. You will need to crack a coconut open using a hammer on a hard surface. But, first, take the water out. For this, punch one of the "eyes" you will find at the bottom of the coconut, and pour the water out into a bowl.

- **Nori Flakes** — Nori is a type of seaweed pressed into a sheet. The Japanese use it to make sushi. Nori flakes are available at health food stores. If you can't find them, use dulse flakes.

- **Spirulina** (powder or flakes) — Spirulina is often sold as a nutritional supplement, when it's actually a food — a super-food! It is not to be confused with blue-green algae. Spirulina is a nutritious algae that can be bought in powdered form or flakes. The flakes contain some lecithin but are still minimally processed.

- **Sprouted Beans** (lentils, mung beans, etc.) — Sprouted lentils, as well as other types of sprouted grains and beans, are made easily at home. Simply soak your lentils (or other types of grains and beans) overnight. Then, rinse them twice a day in a bowl. They will slowly sprout and be ready to eat in 3-4 days (after the soaking night). A good book to learn more on the subject is *The Sprouting Book*, by Ann Wigmore.

- **Sundried Tomatoes** — Salt and preservatives are usually added to sundried tomatoes. Purchase them at health food stores, or make them yourself in your dehydrator. They have to be soaked in warm water for at least an hour before use. If you are in a hurry, soak them for 5-10 minutes in hot water.

- **Sunflower Greens** — Sunflower seeds in the shell sprouted and grown in soil become, after a week, a vegetable that we call sunflower greens. They are now available in many health food stores. Their flavor is full and earthy. You can easily grow them yourself at home. For more information, consult *The Sprouting Book* by Ann Wigmore, or other books on sprouting.

- **Tahini** — Tahini is a nut butter made exclusively from sesame seeds. Though not absolutely raw, because some heat is involved in the process, its occasional, moderate use is beneficial. You can also make your own tahini by grinding hulled sesame seeds in a coffee grounder or heavy-duty blender, and then adding some cold-pressed sesame oil to the mixture.

- **Vanilla (Real)** — Whole vanilla bean (or pods) can be found in health food stores. Otherwise, use some alcohol-free vanilla extract.

- **Young Coconut** — Young coconut (also called "green coconut" or "Thai coconut") is a coconut that has been picked while still young and green. The flesh inside has not had time to harden and the nut contains a lot more juice, which is also sweeter. You can find young coconuts in most Asian markets of major cities in North America.

What Seasonings to Use?
What Seasonings to Avoid?

As I explained in my book, *The Raw Secrets*, it is best to limit the use of most condiments such as salt, spices, hot peppers and some herbs, because of their irritating nature. In this recipe book, I wanted to keep my creations simple, but at the same time be appropriate to a large number of people. Whether you are trying to increase your raw-to-cooked food intake ratio, transitioning from elaborate raw recipes to simple ones, or looking for basic recipe guidelines in order to take the plunge into raw eating (or know someone who is), this handy little book will serve all of the above and more. Therefore, I have used a few seasonings, which are sometimes listed as optional.

There are some seasonings, which are popular in vegetarian recipe books, that you will not find in this book.
These include:

• **Apple cider vinegar**, or other types of vinegar. —
All types of vinegar are quite acid forming. They often encourage fermentation and delay digestion. Instead of using vinegar, use lemon or lime juice. Lemon juice is alkaline forming (despite its acid taste)and does not complicate digestion the way vinegar does.

• **Bragg's Liquid Aminos** — This is a non-fermented soy sauce. Even though there is no salt added, this sauce is quite salty. The company won't tell us how they make it — which is very suspicious.

• **Tamari Sauce and Nama Shoyu** — They are both made from cooked, fermented soy beans. The problem with their use is that they contain a lot of salt.

The Seasonings I Have Used In This Booklet Are:

• **Fresh Herbs** — Fresh herbs may be used. These include dill, basil, cilantro, parsley, etc.

• **Garlic** —Garlic contains mustard oil which irritates the digestive tract. However, it really adds a wonderful taste to some foods. I will occasionally use it in some recipes, making sure that I remove the inside green germ.
According to the French, the inside part of garlic, where the germ is, is what causes bad breath and digestive problems. You can remove it before using garlic and enjoy the flavor without some of the inconveniences.

• **Ginger** — Ginger is a spicy rhizome. A little slice will add a lot of flavor in some recipes.

- **Green Onions** — Green onions are mild and the mustard oil they contain is quickly oxidized when we blend or chop them.
They may be used in small quantities when we want to add more taste to raw soups and salads.

- **Sea Salt** — I want my recipes to be tasty and appeal to a large number of people. For this reason, I have included sea salt as an optional seasoning in some of my recipes. It will please those not used to eating without seasonings and spices. As you feel ready for it, you can use less salt when making your own soups and salads.

- **Sea Vegetables** — Sea vegetables, also called seaweed, include dulse, nori, kelp, etc. They may be used to add flavor and nutrition. They naturally contain some sea salt, but much less than popular salty seasonings. I, personally, eat seaweed regularly, but in moderation. Most natural hygienists are militant against seaweed, while many raw-foodists are militant in its favor. I think that seaweed is a good food, but I try not to abuse it. You can find seaweed in most health food stores, or order it on the Internet (check out my website for resources).

- **Dried Herbs** — Dried herbs, such as thyme, basil, etc., may be used in small quantities. They are fairly mild. It is best to use them fresh.

Raw Soups

Blended foods such as raw soups are easy to prepare and may be helpful for those with digestive problems. A concentrated meal, they are easy to digest when eaten in small quantities. They give the body a rest while providing it with easy-to-assimilate nutrients.

Raw soups are also perfect winter foods, when the body requires nutrients that are more concentrated. You may them slightly warm them up if desired, although most soups will taste better at room temperature.

How to Make Raw Soups

A raw soup basically consists of vegetables, such as tomatoes, cucumbers, celery, lettuce, zucchini, etc. Blend with some liquid, cream with some fatty ingredients — such as avocado, a little oil, or a few nuts — and flavor with some seaweed, lemon juice, mild spices, etc.

I found that in making a typical soup, I blend together the following:

Non-Sweet Fruit — I like to use some non-sweet fruits, such as tomato, zucchini, cucumber, or pepper, because they are high in water, have little fiber and, when blended to a liquid, form a good soup base.

Greens — I often blend lettuce, kale, sprouted sunflower greens, spinach, parsley, and other vegetables into the soup to give it both taste and a nutritional boost. I always try to make sure my soups are not too bitter. Besides green vegetables, you may also blend in some hard vegetables that will add a thicker consistency to the soup, such as carrots, broccoli, or celeriac.

Liquid —The need for adding liquid into raw soups depends on the quantity of non-sweet fruits being used. But most of the time I use very little liquid. Distilled water, coconut water, or vegetable juice are the most common liquids I use. If you use a Vita-mix or other heavy-duty blender, you will have to use very little liquid. If you use a regular blender, you will have to use more in order to be able to blend. You can also use carrot and celery juice (and other vegetable juices) as a base for the soup.

Fatty Ingredients — I may use something to provide creaminess. Generally, I use one type of fatty food. These may include: avocado, young coconut, tahini, nut butter, ground seeds, olive oil, cold-pressed flax seed oil, etc.

Sweet Ingredients — Occasionally, I use coconut water as a liquid. That way, there is something sweet in the soup. In addition to, or in place of, the coconut water, I may add one-half to one apple or pear, but I generally don't use other types of fruit.

Salty-Savory Ingredient — I often add a sea vegetable such as kelp powder, nori flakes, or dulse. I may also use a lot of celery to make the soup saltier. Tomatoes are also salty. In some of the recipes, you will also find some sea salt. This is to add taste to the soup. I always make sure I don't add too much salt to the soup.

Spicy Ingredient — I generally do not use spices, but I often blend a few green onions or a little bit of leeks. The blending process oxidizes most of the strong mustard oil contained in those vegetables. I may also chop a green onion and add it in to the soup, after blending, for taste and presentation.

Tangy Ingredient — I may add some lime or lemon juice to the soup. Tomatoes can also provide a tangy bite to the soup.

Remember that it is sometimes good to let one flavor dominate. If you make a cilantro soup, it should taste like cilantro. All of the other ingredients are then interesting background flavors, but the main flavor is the cilantro. If you make a soup and call it a cucumber soup, it should taste like cucumber.

Another thing that I sometimes like to do is to add solid ingredients into the bowl after the soup has been blended. The ingredients may be stirred into the soup, or left floating on top as a garnish. These solid ingredients may include: chopped avocado, chopped onions, zucchini spirals or grated vegetables. Adding these types of ingredients to a soup can make it heartier, more satisfying, and more interesting.

I created many of these soup recipes using a Vita-Mix, which has a large container. If you don't have a heavy-duty blender and are not ready to purchase one, you will still be able to make the recipes in this book. For some raw soups, you may have to blend half of the quantities first, pour it into a bowl, and then blend the other half. You will also have to blend for a longer period.

What Blender to Use

There are many types of blenders available on the market. But, in actuality, we have two types: the household blender and the heavy-duty blender. I recommend that you get a heavy-duty blender. The difference is similar to buying a cheap pair of shoes from Wal-Mart that you will have to change after a few months — while walking without comfort and hurting your feet at the same time — or buying a quality pair of choose that will give you complete satisfaction and last you several years.

There is of course a steep difference in price. While you can get a cheap blender for $50, a heavy-duty blender usually goes for $400. It's expensive, but well worth the money. It will last you a lifetime (they usually have a warranty of at least seven years), when a cheap blender will often break after a few months of heavy use, without giving you the results you should expect from a blender.

A heavy duty blender can hold twice as much as a regular blender, can blend hard fruits and vegetables into a puree without even needing to add water, and can even grind grains and turn them into a flour (with the proper attachment). In ten seconds, you can have a smoothie or a raw soup; with a cheap blender, it will be a long, often hazardous operation.

With a heavy-duty blender, you can create not only soups, smoothies, and salad dressing, but also pudding, ice-cream, and the like — all from fruits and vegetables!

I've never regretted the few hundred dollars I have spent for my Vita-Mix. There are other good heavy-duty blenders available on the market today, the Vita-Mix being the most well known. Many restaurants, juice bars, and raw-foodists use it.

If you budget is limited and you decide to buy a regular blender, make sure that you get one with a large container.

How Does It Work?

Tbs. means tablespoon
tsp. means teaspoon

The order of the ingredient is roughly the order in which you should put foods into the blender.

Don't try to blend everything at once. Instead, blend the first few ingredients, which form the base of the soup, and then add the rest progressively.

Raw Soup Recipes

Green Romaine Soup

1/3 to 1/2 cup water
1/2 lemon juice
1 tomato
1 small cucumber
2 cups romaine lettuce leaves
1/2 apple
1/2 avocado
2 green onions
2 Tbs. nori flakes (optional)

Blend everything, pour into a bowl.

Add the following:

1 cup alfalfa or clover sprouts, chopped
1/2 avocado, diced
1 green onion, chopped

Mix everything together and serve.

Djitsu Cream

3 tomatoes
4 Tbs. water
1/2 lemon, juice of
12 black sundried olives, pitted
1/3 cup fresh parsley
1 green onion

Blend everything together and serve. Don't forget to take the pits out of the olives! The flavors in this soup are intense. With no water and less tomatoes, it could be served as a dip.

Asparagus Soup

1/2 cup water
1 cup carrots, diced
1 cup asparagus
1-2 Tbs. olive oil
1 tsp. sweet paprika powder
1 clove garlic
pinch sea salt (to taste)

Start by blending the carrots and water until smooth, and then add the asparagus progressively. Blend everything and serve. Add sea salt to taste.

Popeye Cream

1 large tomato, diced
1/2 orange or tangerine, juice of
4 cups of spinach
1/2 inch fresh ginger
2 green onions
1 avocados
1 pinch sea salt (optional)

Blend the tomato and orange juice, and then add the spinach progressively. Blend with the other ingredients. Add water only if necessary. This is a nice green soup!

Dill Soup

1 lemon, juice of
3 medium tomatoes
1 zucchini, peeled
1/2 small cucumber
3 ribs of celery
1 cup fresh dill
1 avocado
2 Tbs. olive oil (optional)
1 clove garlic
1/2 tsp. sea salt (optional)

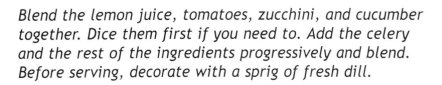

Blend the lemon juice, tomatoes, zucchini, and cucumber together. Dice them first if you need to. Add the celery and the rest of the ingredients progressively and blend. Before serving, decorate with a sprig of fresh dill.

Celery-Avocado Cream

1 1/2 cup water
3 cups celery, chopped
2 avocados
1 clove garlic

Blend everything, starting with the water and celery, and then adding the avocados and other ingredients. This is a very mild, smooth soup.

Cabby Soup

1/2 cup water (or more if needed)
1 cup red cabbage
2 ribs of celery
1/2 cup peeled zucchini
1/2 apple (small)
1/2 lemon, juice of
1 Tbs. olive oil (optional)
1 avocado

Blend everything. This is a sweet, smooth soup recipe.

Light Summer Kale Soup

3 tomatoes (small to medium)
1 cup water (or more)
1 cup of romaine lettuce
1 1/2 cups kale leaves
1/2 Fuji apple
2 Tbs. lemon juice
1/4 cups fresh basil
1/2 cup fresh coriander
1 inch fresh ginger
1 avocado
pinch sea salt (to taste)

Blend everything. Garnish with chopped onions (I personally chop onions and let them air-dry for about 48 hours. They then become sweeter and less strong.).

Carrot Delight

2 cups carrot juice
1 cup celery juice
1/2 lemon, juice of
1 cup of zucchini
1 avocado
1 handful whole-leaf dulse, briefly rinsed
1 inch ginger
1 clove garlic

Add but don't blend:

1 and 1/2 cups of grated zucchini

First make the carrot and celery juice in your juicer, or buy some freshly made at a juice bar. Blend with the other ingredients. At the end, add the grated zucchini, but don't blend. Mix well and serve. This is a great soup to serve as an entree.

Cream of Broccoli

1 cup water
1/2 lemon, juice of
2 cups broccoli, chopped
1/2 cup pecan nuts
1 green onion
pinch sea salt (to taste)

Blend the water, lemon juice, and broccoli together until smooth. Add the other ingredients. Add sea salt to taste. This soup is rather strong. With less water, it could be used as a dressing.

Italy

1/2 cup water
2 cups tomato, chopped
1/3 cup fresh parsley
1/3 cup fresh cilantro
1/4 cup fresh basil
2 green onions
1 clove garlic
2 Tbs. olive oil
pinch sea salt (to taste)

Blend the water and tomatoes. Add the rest of the ingredients progressively. Serve with a sprig of parsley.

Red Stuff

1/4 cup water
juice of l/2 lemon
1 small cucumber
2 small to medium red bell peppers, chopped
1 green onion
1/3 cup fresh parsley
1/3 cup fresh cilantro
1 garlic clove
pinch sea salt (to taste)

Blend the water, lemon juice, red bell pepper and cucumber together until smooth. Then add all of the other ingredients and blend.

Butternut Soup

1 and 1/2 cups water
2 cups butternut squash, diced
4 ribs of celery
2 Tbs. tahini
2 green onions
1/2 cup fresh basil
1/2 tsp. sea salt
1/2 tsp. paprika

Blend the water and half of the butternut squash. Add progressively the other half as well as the rest of the ingredients and blend. This is a sweet soup that will surprise more than one. It is ideally made using a heavy-duty blender such as the Vita-Mix.

Green Cuke

6 small cucumbers, peeled and chopped
2 green onions
1/4 cup fresh dill
1/4 cup fresh parsley
3 cups romaine lettuce
2 avocados
pinch of sea salt (to taste)

Blend the cucumbers together, adding water only if you really need to. Add the rest of the ingredients progressively. You have to try this one out!

Beautiful Beet Soup

1 1/4 cups of water
juice of one lemon
1 small red bell pepper
1 small beet, peeled and diced
1 cup of kohlrabi, peeled and diced
1 rib of celery
1/2 avocado
2 Tbs. dulse flakes

Blend all of the ingredients together. Serve this delicious, fresh soup as an entree. Kohlrabi is a member of the turnip family, also called cabbage turnip.

Blended Salad

3 tomatoes, roughly chopped
2 ribs of celery
4 leaves lettuce (big)
1 cup handful spinach
1 green onion
1/2 avocado
1/4 cup parsley
2 Tbs. dulse flakes
1 Tbs. nori flakes (optional)
water if needed

Blend the tomatoes together, ad add the rest of the ingredients progressively. Use water only if you need to. A blended salad should be quite thick.

Blended Salad #2

2 cups of baby greens mix
1 tomato
1/2 cucumber
1 rib of celery
juice 1/2 lemon
1/2 red bell pepper
1 avocado

Blend all of the ingredients and keep the consistency thick. You can find a baby greens mix in most health food stores and supermarkets.

How to Make a Great Salad

The key to making a good salad that will please everyone is to be inventive while keeping it simple. Being inventive means using vegetables and ingredients you normally wouldn't think of using, and in new, original combinations.

Here are some vegetables people don't think of using in salads, but that could form a great base for them. I have used them in some of the recipes in this book.

- **Fennel** — Fennel has a wonderful aroma and is excellent raw in salads.

- **Jícama** — Pronounce: Hi-ka-ma. This root-vegetable is popular in Mexico and in some Asian countries. The taste is a mix between the potato and the apple.

- **Fresh raw corn (on the cob)** — Fresh raw corn is excellent. It has to be at least 24 hours fresh, so only use it in season and locally.

- **Sprouted beans** — sprouted beans, such as lentils and mung beans, add something to a salad. I don't make the base out of them, because they are too concentrated, but they form a nice addition to the salad.

- **Various sprouts** — Green sprouts, such as sunflower or buckwheat, as well as alfalfa, clover, etc., are essential ingredients of the daily vegetable salad.

- **Celeriac** — Celeriac is a weird-looking root vegetable related to celery. It is popular in Europe and less in North America. Now, it can be found in most major markets and health food stores. Its flavor is delicate and can be compared to a mix between celery and parsley.

In each salad, you usually want to add some of these tastes:

Sweet - Adding some sweetness to a salad doesn't necessarily involve putting dates or fruit in it. It may be just a touch of sweetness that the salad needs. Tomatoes are sweet. So are red bell peppers (or other colored bell peppers). Sundried tomatoes also fit that description. What else can add sweetness to the salad? Fresh corn, beets, apples, carrots, walnuts and other nuts.

Spicy — We like a little bite to the salad, so that's why people put onions in them. My choices, since I don't want to use strong spices, are chopped green onions, chopped onions in small quantities (chopping it oxidizes a lot of the irritant mustard oil) and garlic.

Oily —I like salads to be filling, so I usually add some type of fatty food to it. It may be cold-pressed oil, avocado, nuts, or olives. I almost never mix nuts and avocados together because they do not combine very well.

Savory — Some vegetables are quite salty on their own, such as celery, tomatoes, etc. You may also use seaweed or a pinch of sea salt.

Tangy — A typical salad is drowned in vinegar, which turns it into quite an unhealthy mixture. Instead of vinegar, I use lemon juice, lime juice, sometimes grapefruit or orange juice (in small quantities), tomatoes, etc.

You want to limit the ingredients in the salad. Better to limit the number of vegetables to 4-6 types, and instead vary the salads each day.

To make dressings, you've got two possibilities. You can either put the "dressing ingredients" directly inside the salad bowl, and mix them with the vegetables, or make the dressing separately, and add it to the salad when serving it. I prefer the former method to the latter, but that also depends of what type of salad I am preparing. The following recipes use both techniques.

Another important point: try to chop the ingredients small, or at least the same size. Beginners don't know that, but chefs do. Don't have big pieces of lettuce in the salad if everything else is chopped small. Otherwise, you won't taste the flavors. Have everything chopped approximately at the same size.

For more information on the art of salad making, consult my book *The Sunfood Cuisine*.

Salad Recipes

Summer Fun

2 cups fresh raw corn, kernels only
2 big tomatoes, chopped
2 cups of romaine lettuce, chopped
2 cups of raw mango, diced
pinch sea salt (optional)

This is a summer recipe, to be prepared during harvest time. Mix all ingredients together. Get the freshest corn and the tastiest tomatoes: this is the only way to make this recipe. Simple and delicious.

Fennel Delights

3 cups of fennel, thinly sliced
1/4 cup chopped parsley
1 yellow pepper, diced
1 celery rib, diced
1/2 avocado, diced
2 Tbs. olive oil
6-8 sundried tomatoes, soaked and chopped

Soak the sundried tomatoes in advance for at least one hour. Mix all of the ingredients and be prepared for something delicious!

Winter Fort

1 cup peeled, grated beet
1 cup grated zucchini
1 cup grated red cabbage
1 small apple, peeled and diced
2 ribs of celery, diced
2 cups sprouted lentils, or mung beans (home-made)
2 Tbs. olive oil
1 lemon, juice of
pinch sea salt (optional)

Mix all of the ingredients together and ideally let sit for sometime for the flavors to mix. For this recipe, use sprouted mung beans that you sprout at home, not those you buy at the store. The home-sprouted mung beans are starchier, which is what is needed for this recipe. You may also use sprouted lentils. This is a great winter recipe.

Celery Salad

4 cups of celery, sliced thinly
2 avocados, diced
2 cups sprouts (alfalfa or clover)
1/2 black radish, shredded
2 Tbs. dulse flakes

The celery has to be sliced as thinly as possible. Then mix with the other ingredients. Make sure that you peel the black radish. This is quite a filling salad, for times when you feel like something consistent.

Broccoli Salad

4 cups broccoli, chopped
1 yellow bell pepper, diced
1/4 cup parsley, chopped

Dressing:

1/4 cup water
1 lemon, juice of
1 avocado
1 rib of celery
1/2 tsp. sea salt

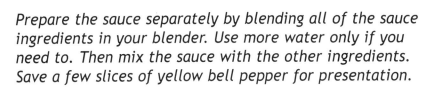

Prepare the sauce separately by blending all of the sauce ingredients in your blender. Use more water only if you need to. Then mix the sauce with the other ingredients. Save a few slices of yellow bell pepper for presentation.

Cauliflower-Avocado

1 small head of cauliflower, shredded
1 avocado, mashed
15 sun-dried, black olives, pitted and chopped
1 red pepper, diced small
1/2 lemon, juice of
1/4 cup chopped parsley
1 clove garlic

You can shred the cauliflower in your food processor, or by hand. Then mix with the other ingredients. This is a filling salad.

Frédéric's Favorite

1/2 head of lettuce
1 handful of arugula, chopped
2-3 small tomatoes, diced
1-2 Tbs. lemon juice
1 avocado, diced
2 green onions, chopped
dulse flakes, or whole dulse, rinsed and chopped (to taste)

This is my favorite salad for when I feel like something filling and savory. Use dulse flakes to taste. I prefer to rinse a good handful of whole dulse, chop it, and add it to the salad.

Winter Roots

1 1/3 cups grated carrots
2/3 cup grated beets
1 1/3 cups grated celeriac
2 celery ribs, chopped
2 Tbs. grated white onion

Mix everything together. Grating the onion oxidizes most of the strong mustard oil. There are two possibilities of dressings for this salad:

Avocado Dressing:

8 Tbs. water
1 lemon, juice of
1 tomato
1 avocado
pinch of sea salt (optional)

Blend everything and mix with the salad.

or,

Tahini sauce:

8 Tbs. water
1 tomato
1 lemon, juice of
6 Tbs. tahini
pinch of sea salt (optional)

Blend everything and mix with the salad. The salad should be drowned in dressing!

Fred's Fun Salad

1/2 head of lettuce, or mixed greens, chopped
1 yellow bell pepper, diced
2 ribs of celery, chopped
2 medium tomatoes, diced
1 avocado, diced or mashed
1 Tbs. of olive oil (optional)
1 handful rinsed whole-leaf dulse, chopped
1/4 lemon, juice of

This is another favorite, similar to Fred's Favorite (in fact, it may well be my favorite, I don't know!). Simply mix all of the ingredients together. Dulse should be briefly rinsed, to remove some of its saltiness but not all of it.

Kohlrabi Baby

2 cups of kohlrabi, peeled and shredded
2 Tbs. of fresh basil, minced
1/4 cup of fresh cilantro, chopped

Dressing:

1/4 cup water
1/2 lemon, juice of
1 avocado
2 stalks of celery
pinch of sea salt (to taste)

You need to peel the kohlrabi, then, shred with a vegetable shredder or a food processor. Mix all of the ingredients in a bowl, and add the dressing separately. For the dressing, blend all of the dressing ingredients in your blender, adding more water only if you need to. Add sea salt to taste.

Simple Delight

3 cups of spring salad mix (baby greens)
1 cup of home-sprouted mung beans
1 1/2 cups peeled, thinly sliced zucchini

Dressing:

1/2 lemon, juice of
4 tsp. olive oil
1/2 t. paprika
2 pinches sea salt (to taste)

The baby greens salad mix can be found in most health food stores, and even in some supermarkets. Mix all of the ingredients together. For the dressing, simply mix the dressing ingredients in a cup or a bowl. Add sea salt to taste.

Light Salad

2 cups peeled and shredded zucchini
1 cup shredded carrots
2 cups of baby greens salad mix

Dressing:

4 Tbs. water
2 Tbs. tahini
3 Tbs. lemon juice
1 tsp. minced ginger

For this recipe, prepare the dressing separately in a bowl. You simply mix everything by hand with a spoon, and add the dressing to the salad.

Filling Stuff

4-5 cups lettuce, chopped
2 tomatoes, chopped
10 kalamatha olives, pitted and chopped
2 Tbs. kalamatha olive juice
1/2 cup walnuts, chopped

Mix everything together. The kalamatha olive juice is simply the liquid found in the container of kalamatha olives. You can find these olives in many markets that sell olives.

Macaroni

Sauce:

4 medium tomatoes, chopped
20-24 sundried tomatoes halves
1 apple (small), peeled
1 lemon, juice of
1 clove garlic

Mix with:

8-10 cups mung beans (store-bought), chopped

First prepare the sauce by blending all of the ingredients together (except for the mung beans). If you don't use a heavy-duty blender, you will have to let the sundried tomatoes soak for some time beforehand (a few hours). Use more or less sun-dried tomatoes to reach a thick, tomato sauce consistency.

Then pour mix the sauce along with the chopped mung beans. These are the sprouted mung beans that we buy at the store (people make Chop Suey with them). There is no way really to make sprouted beans like that at home, unless you know the secret technique (and I don't).

Smoothies

Smoothies are fun food. You can use different types of fruit and blend them into a drink or a "pudding." Smoothies are a great way to start the day. They take only a few minutes to prepare, and will provide you with something substantial that can last for a few hours. I usually recommend them to all those starting on the raw path. Smoothies will impress your friends and family who have a sweet tooth (who doesn't?). And the best thing is that you don't have to be a genius to make them, nor do you have to use sugar and artificial ingredients.

What Goes Into a Smoothie?

I have made some breakthroughs lately in my smoothie-making technique. I have found that I could add soft vegetables such as lettuce or celery to the smoothies for added taste and nutrition. But generally, smoothies are made of different fruits. We can also add nuts, seeds, or oil to them. If I add some nuts or oil to a smoothies, I make sure it is in small amounts. Soaked nuts or young coconuts will be easier to digest than dry nuts when mixed into a smoothie.

The ingredients that can make up a smoothie are:

- Fresh fruit
- Bananas
- Frozen bananas (to create a "milk shake")
- Dates (to sweeten)
- Dried figs or other dried fruits (to sweeten)
- Celery or lettuce (to add taste and nutrition)
- Sprouts (for taste adventurers)
- Real vanilla, or alcohol-free vanilla extract
- Carob powder (for a chocolate taste)
- Coconut water
- Young coconut (to give some consistency)
- Soaked or dried nuts and seeds
- Durian (for a real taste experience)
- Spirulina (for a "green smoothie")

Smoothie Recipes

Papaya pudding

1 medium papaya (about 2 cups)
2 oranges
3 dates

Blend everything together, adding water only if you really need to. This is a very delicious pudding recipe.

Sunflower-Banana Smoothie

1 cup water
3 bananas
1 dried fig
1 and 1/2 cups sunflower greens, or lettuce

This smoothie has a very earthy taste. If you are not a taste adventurer, beware...

Pineapple Fred

1/2 pineapple, gold and ripe
1 mango
1 papaya

Blend everything. It goes without saying that peels and seeds don't go in there!

Durian Pudding

2 cups of durian
coconut water
1 centimeter real vanilla, or 3-4 drops of vanilla extract (optional)

Blend with just enough coconut water to reach a pudding consistency. If you don't have a heavy-duty blender, you could try making this recipe in a food processor. A blender can also work. If you can't find real vanilla, use a few drops of natural vanilla extract.

Hey Dude

1 cup water
2 bananas
12 almonds
5 dates, pitted
1 centimeter real vanilla, or 3-4 drops of vanilla extract

Blend until smooth. The almonds give a really nice taste. If you can't find real vanilla, use a few drops of natural vanilla extract.

Chocolate Shake

1 cup water
2 cups durian
2 Tbs. carob powder
6 dates, pitted

Blend everything. This pudding will impress you.

Coco-Nutso

2 red delicious apples (or other sweet variety)
1 1/2 cups coconut water (from mature coconuts)
6-8 dates, pitted
a piece of 4 by 4 inches of mature coconut meat

Blend everything until you reach a smooth consistency. This is a sweet, very yummy smoothie recipe. Be sure to use mature coconuts, which can be found in most supermarkets. Beware, sometimes they are too old and the water inside is bad! Better to buy them at Asian markets. If your blender can't handle blending the mature coconut meat, shred it beforehand.

Day Starter

1 cup of water
2 oranges
1 apple
3 dates

Blend everything.

Sweet Paste

2 oranges
1 apple
2 ribs of celery
3 dried figs

Blend everything. Be sure to remove the stems from the figs. You can also soak them beforehand.

Miss Sevilla

1 mango
2 bananas, ripe
1 pear

Blend. Use a little water if you need to.

Banana Slug

1 1/2 cups water.
2 bananas
1 mango
1 cup romaine lettuce

Blend everything. If you think lettuce and bananas can't combine, think again!

Mango-Coco

2 slices pineapple (about 3 inches)
1 big mango
1 cup coconut water from mature coconut

Blend everything. Be sure to use mature coconuts for the water, to give this nice coconut taste. If you don't have coconut water, simply use water and add two dates.

White Coconut

2 cups coconut water
2 bananas
1 young coconut, meat of
1 inch real vanilla

Blend everything. Use young coconuts for this recipe. If you can't find real vanilla, use a few drops of natural vanilla extract.

Carob Smoothie

2 cups coconut water
2 bananas
1 young coconut, meat of
2 Tbs. carob powder
6-8 dates, pitted

Blend everything. This is a variation of the previous recipe, but turning it into a carob smoothie.

Lemon-Durian Pudding

2 cups thawed frozen durian (still cold)
2 Tbs. lemon juice
1 cup water

Blend everything and prepare for something delicious! Who would think that durian and lemon mix well together? Well, they do. Be sure to use frozen durian for this recipe. Let it thaw in warm water for about one hour.

Yellow-O

1 cup water
1 banana, fresh or frozen
1 big mango
2 cups thawed frozen durian (still cold)
1 inch of real vanilla

Blend everything. Yes, yes, you can mix durian with other fruits, especially in a smoothie. If you can't find real vanilla, use a few drops of natural vanilla extract. Impress your friends with this recipe.

Coco-Mango

1 young coconut, meat of
1 cup coconut water (or more)
2 mangoes, diced

Blend everything.

Green Spirulina Smoothie

1 cup water
1 cup papaya
1 large mango
1-2 tsp. spirulina powder (or flakes)

Blend everything together and be prepared for something delicious. This is my favorite smoothie recipe of all time (inspired by my friend Surya's recipe)!

Best Coconut Smoothie

water of one young coconut
6-8 dried black mission figs
1 banana
meat 1/2 young coconut (optional)

If you don't have a heavy-duty blender, soak the black mission figs before hand, and blend them with their soaking water. In this case, use less coconut water to keep the same consistency. This is a very sweet dessert recipe.

Extra Section: Raw Dips

The following recipes can be made using a food processor, which will work better than a Vita-Mix or a blender. They are dips which can all be served with vegetables as entrees or part of a complete meal.

Special Hummus

2 cups peeled zucchini, chopped
4 Tbs. olive oil
1 and 1/2 lemon, juice of
3/4 cup sesame seeds (hulled)
3/4 tsp. sea salt
2 garlic cloves
1 tsp. paprika

Blend all of the ingredients in your Vita-Mix or food processor. Be sure that you use hulled sesame seeds, which are white. If you use a food processor, you should grind the seeds beforehand in a coffee grounder. Serve with vegetables.

Pretty Guacamole

1 avocado
1/2 medium tomato
1 green onion
1 clove garlic
1/2 lemon, juice of
1/3 tsp. sea salt (optional)

Blend all of the ingredients in your food processor or blender.

Add to the mixture:

1 tomato, chopped
4-6 sundried tomato halves, soaked and diced small

Mix everything well together. Serve with sliced vegetables, and dip like chips.

Burrito Dip

1 cup walnuts
1/2 lemon, juice of
2 tsp. chili powder (organic)
2 Tsb. chopped onion
1 large red bell pepper, diced
1/2 cup sun-dried tomatoes, soaked and diced

Mix all of the ingredients in your food processor. First, liquefy the walnuts and lemon juice, then add the other ingredients, and keep on mixing in your food processor, but without blending. Serve inside green lettuce leaves.

Fun Guacamole

1 avocado
1 cup green beans, chopped
1/2 lemon, juice of
1 inch of grated ginger
1 clove garlic
1 tsp. curry
1/4 cup chopped cilantro
2 Tbs. dulse flakes

Mix all of the ingredients except the last two in your food processor to achieve a smooth consistency. Then add the chopped cilantro and dulse flakes. Mix well and serve.

Avocado Mayonnaise

1 avocado
1/2 lemon, juice of
2 Tbs. dulse flakes
1 tsp. curry powder
1 tsp. honey or maple syrup, or 2 dates

In your food processor, blend the avocado with lemon juice, and add the oil progressively as well as the other ingredients. This is an excellent dip, salad dressing, or sauce for "nori rolls."

Easy Dip

2 avocados
1 large red bell pepper
1/2 orange, juice of
1/2 lemon, juice of
2 Tbs. dulse flakes

Mix everything in your blender or food processor.

Super-Duper Green Spirulina Guacamole

2 avocados
1 lemon, juice of
1 cup arugula, finely chopped
2 medium tomatoes, diced
2-3 tsp. spirulina powder, or spirulina flakes

Mash the avocados in a bowl, or run them through your food processor, along with the lemon juice. Add the other ingredients. Serve inside lettuce leaves, or as a dip with vegetables. Spirulina is a great food to add to guacamole to give it a boost.

Now that you've bought Raw Soups

Frederic has weekly, politically-incorrect health & nutrition news for you!

Are you looking for:

- Exclusive interview with top authorities and unique thinkers in the field
- Informative and thought-provoking articles
- Useful advice and tips
- The latest relevant research, not just the newest fad

You'll find all of that and more in the
Pure Health & Nutrition E-Zine

All of this is absolutely free!

TO SUBSCRIBE TO MY WEEKLY E-NEWSLETTER

"PURE HEALTH AND NUTRITION"

Visit my website (click on "Newsletter"):

www.fredericpatenaude.com

About the Author

Frederic Patenaude has been working in the natural health movement since 1998, and has a wealth of experience in the field of nutrition, health and personal development. He is the author of seven books, including The Raw Secrets and his articles are read by tens of thousands of people every week.

Frederic spends his time between his home country of Canada and a part of the year in a tropical location like Hawaii or Thailand.

He lives in Vancouver with his wife and their likeable cat, Xander.

Other books & courses from or published by Frederic

For a complete list of available books and products, and to free subscription to Fred's outrageous health and wellness tips, as well as Fred's e-mail tips on making a living doing what you love, by going to, go to: www.fredericpatenaude.com

Other Books by the Author Include:

- The Raw Secrets: The Raw Food Diet in the Real World
- Raw Food Controversies
- The Sunfood Cuisine
- Instant Raw Sensations
- The Perfect Health Program

For a complete list of available products, go to
www.fredericpatenaude.com

Made in the USA
Charleston, SC
02 April 2013